SUMMER FUN

THE CORNER KIDS

Written by Larry Dane Brimner • Illustrated by Christine Tripp

Children's Press®
A Division of Scholastic Inc.
New York • Toronto • London • Auckland • Sydney
Mexico City • New Delhi • Hong Kong
Danbury, Connecticut

For Charlie and Allison
—L.D.B.

For my pal, Julie
—C.T.

Reading Consultants
Linda Cornwell
Literacy Specialist

Katharine A. Kane
Education Consultant
(Retired, San Diego County Office of Education and San Diego State University)

Library of Congress Cataloging-in-Publication Data

Brimner, Larry Dane.
  Summer fun / written by Larry Dane Brimner ; illustrated by Christine Tripp.
        p. cm. — (Rookie choices)
  Summary: When the Corner Kids cannot go to the water park because the car breaks down, Alex figures out a way they can have fun in spite of their disappointment.
  ISBN 0-516-22548-0 (lib. bdg.)   0-516-27836-3 (pbk.)
  [1. Disappointment—Fiction. 2. Play—Fiction.] I. Tripp, Christine, ill. II. Title. III. Series.
  PZ7.B767 Su 2003
  [E]—dc21

                                    2002015579

CHILDREN'S PRESS, AND ROOKIE CHOICES™, and associated logos are trademarks and or registered trademarks of Grolier Publishing Co., Inc. SCHOLASTIC and associated logos are trademarks and or registered trademarks of Scholastic Inc.
1 2 3 4 5 6 7 8 9 10 R 12 11 10 09 08 07 06 05 04 03

This book is about **cheerfulness.**

Alex, Gabby, and Three J could hardly wait. They were going to Wild Water Park for some cool, summer fun.

The Corner Kids piled in the car.
The three friends called themselves
the Corner Kids because they
lived on opposite corners of
the same street.

Alex's mom turned the car key.

The car rattled and shook. *Bang!* Then it got quiet and still.

"It's not starting," said Alex's mom.

The Corner Kids looked worried. "How come?" asked Alex.

9

His mom shook her head and told everyone to pile out of the car. Then she called for help.

11

Later, a tow truck pulled away from the curb. Alex watched his mom's car roll down the street behind it.

"Sorry, you guys," Alex said quietly. "We can't go to the water park."

Gabby hung her head.

Three J looked at his inner tube. "Guess I won't be needing this," he said, sounding grouchy.

15

Alex knew Three J and Gabby wanted to float under a waterfall as much as he did. He felt bad about letting his friends down.

"I know," said Alex. "We can go to the school playground. We can have fun there."

17

"Some fun," Gabby said, sounding sad.

"Might as well go, though," grumbled Three J. "There's nothing else to do."

19

The Corner Kids rolled their
inner tubes to Cottonwood School.
They sat quietly on the lawn.
They watched Mr. Price.
He was watering the roses
in the rose garden.

21

That gave Alex an idea.
He jumped up and talked
with Mr. Price.

Then he joined his
friends again.

23

In no time, the lawn sprinklers began to spray water in all directions.

"Come on, you guys!" called Alex. "Let's have some fun."

25

The Corner Kids darted in and out of the sprinklers. They jumped and splashed. Even Gabby and Three J were having fun.

27

After a while, Gabby sat in her inner tube and stretched her arms in the air. "This is cool!" she shouted.

Three J laughed, and nodded his agreement.

29

Alex smiled at his happy friends. He knew the Corner Kids could have a good time no matter what.

31

ABOUT THE AUTHOR

Larry Dane Brimner studied literature and writing at San Diego State University and taught school for twenty years. The author of more than seventy-five books for children, many of them Children's Press titles, he enjoys meeting young readers and writers when he isn't at his computer.

ABOUT THE ILLUSTRATOR

Christine Tripp lives in Ottawa, Canada, with her husband Don; four grown children—Elizabeth, Erin, Emily, and Eric; son-in-law Jason; grandsons Brandon and Kobe; four cats; and one very large, scruffy puppy named Jake.